P9-DCB-771

Ela Area Public Library District
275 Mohawk Trail, Lake Zurich, IL 60047
(847) 438-3433
www.eapl.org

31241008705561

JUN – – 2016

OUT OF THE LAB
EXTREME JOBS IN SCIENCE

ROCKET SCIENTISTS

Barbara M. Linde

PowerKiDS press.

New York

Published in 2016 by The Rosen Publishing Group, Inc.
29 East 21st Street, New York, NY 10010

Copyright © 2016 by The Rosen Publishing Group, Inc.

Acknowledgements: NASA Langley Research Center: Jeffrey Hinkley, Ronald Krueger, Gretchen Murri, Dan Murri, James Reeder, Patrick Troutman, Julie Williams-Byrd; NASA Marshall Space Flight Center: Carrie Olsen; NASA Wallops Flight Facility; Aerojet Rocketdyne Redmond: Deiter Zube; Colorado Space Grant Consortium: Jesse Austin; Virginia Space Grant Consortium: Kirsten Manning, Brenda Neil.

All rights reserved. No part of this book may be reproduced in any form without permission in writing from the publisher, except by a reviewer.

First Edition

Editor: Katie Kawa
Designer: Mickey Harmon

Photo Credits: Cover (background), p. 7 Bill Ingalls/NASA/Handout/Getty Images News/Getty Images; cover (woman) PathDoc/Shutterstock.com;
p. 4 (rocket launch) Jason and Bonnie Grower/Shutterstock.com; pp. 4–5, 13 (inset), 14, 15, 16, 21, 26–27, 29 Courtesy of NASA; pp. 8–9 Triff/ Shutterstock.com; p. 11 (inset) Sovfoto/Contributor/Universal Images Group/ Getty Images; p. 11 (main) ullstein bild/Contributor/ullstein bild/Getty Images; p. 13 (main) https://en.wikipedia.org/wiki/Goddard_Space_Flight_Center#/media/ File:Goddard_Space_Flight_Center_Visitor%27s_Center.jpg; p. 17 l i g h t p o e t/ Shutterstock.com; pp. 18–19 Universalimagesgroup/Contributor/Universal Images Group/Getty Images; pp. 23–24 Getty Images/Handout/Getty Images News/ Getty Images; pp. 25–26 Wayne0216/Shutterstock.com; p. 28 bikeriderlondon/ Shutterstock.com; p. 30 John A Davis/Shutterstock.com.

Library of Congress Cataloging-in-Publication Data

Linde, Barbara M., author.
 Rocket scientists / Barbara M. Linde.
    pages cm. — (Out of the lab: extreme jobs in science)
 Includes index.
ISBN 978-1-4994-1855-2 (pbk.)
ISBN 978-1-5081-4525-7 (6 pack)
ISBN 978-1-5081-4526-4 (library binding)
1. Rockets (Aeronautics)—Juvenile literature. 2. Astronautics—Vocational guidance—Juvenile literature. 3. Aerospace engineering—Juvenile literature. I. Title.
 TL850.L56 2016
 629.1—dc23
                        2015036917

Manufactured in the United States of America

CPSIA Compliance Information: Batch #BW16PK: For Further Information contact Rosen Publishing, New York, New York at 1-800-237-9932

Contents

IT DOES TAKE A ROCKET SCIENTIST!

You've probably heard the sayings "It doesn't take a rocket scientist to do that" and "This isn't rocket science." However, suppose you want to launch a rocket to look for signs of life in space. Perhaps the astronauts on the **International Space Station** (ISS) need supplies. Closer to home, a company might want to put new **satellites** for television and **GPS** systems into orbit. In these kinds of situations, it really does take a rocket scientist, and it really is rocket science!

Are you curious about how machines work? Are you willing to tackle problems no one has ever attempted before? Then a career as a rocket scientist might be a great fit for you. Read on to learn more about some of the men and women who've chosen this extreme career!

Many rocket scientists work together to make rocket launches possible.

SCIENCE IN ACTION

The National Aeronautics and Space Administration (NASA) is the United States government agency that oversees air and space exploration. Many rocket scientists have jobs with NASA.

WHAT'S A ROCKET?

When you hear the word "rocket," do you think of a large, fiery engine? Maybe you think of a tall, thin **vehicle** that blasts into space? If you think of either of these things, you're right!

A rocket engine doesn't need air to work, so it can work in space. It burns either liquid or solid fuel that turns into gas, which is called exhaust. The action of the gas escaping from the back of the rocket moves the rocket forward. This forward force is called thrust.

Powerful Saturn V rockets carried NASA astronauts on their voyages to the moon. Atlas V, Delta II, and Pegasus rockets launch satellites, **probes**, and space telescopes. Antares rockets now carry supplies to the ISS. Rocket scientists designed and built all these rockets.

Rocket scientists make a rocket launch using a scientific rule called Newton's Third Law of Motion. This law states that for every action, there's an equal and opposite reaction. The rocket pushes the exhaust backward, and the exhaust pushes the rocket in the opposite direction—forward—with equal force.

REACTION

ACTION

SCIENCE IN ACTION

The Chinese were the first to develop rockets around 1200 AD. These rockets were used for fireworks and weapons. Other countries soon followed. Rockets weren't used for other purposes for hundreds of years.

MANY JOBS, ONE TITLE

"Rocket scientist" is a popular term that generally refers to someone who works in the field of aerospace engineering, especially aerospace engineers who deal with rockets. Aerospace engineers use math and science to design, build, test, and operate vehicles that fly. These intelligent, talented people build and launch rockets and guide them in orbit. They also design and build spacecraft such as the ISS. Some rocket scientists are now trying to figure out how humans can travel to Mars and possibly live there.

Many rocket scientists in the United States work directly for NASA. Others work for private companies or universities. Most of these rocket scientists still interact with NASA, too. Other countries, including Japan, Russia, and the United Kingdom, have their own space agencies.

SCIENCE IN ACTION

Rocket scientists sometimes work in **wind tunnels**, testing rockets. Some work on launch pads, which are where rockets are launched into space. Others are astronauts who go into space!

These are some of the many career fields you can choose from if you're interested in a career in aerospace science and engineering.

Aerospace Careers

career field	What do you do at a job in this field?
aerodynamics	study the movement of air around flying vehicles such as rockets and how the vehicles move through the air
propulsion systems	research and test new systems for producing thrust
structural design	plan the way a rocket or other flying vehicle will be built; test those plans
materials	test the materials used to build rockets and other space vehicles to see if they can handle space travel
stability and control systems	study how to control the speed and direction of a rocket or other flying vehicle; design controls for pilots to use
avionics	design the electronic systems used to launch and control aircraft and spacecraft
payload systems	plan and test how a rocket or other flying vehicle will handle its payload, or the cargo and tools it's carrying

TURNING FICTION INTO FACT

Years ago, neither the military nor the science community thought of launching rockets into space, but imaginative writers did!

Jules Verne published his novel *From the Earth to the Moon* in 1865. His characters used rockets to launch and steer a spaceship to travel to the moon. Later experiments showed that the math Verne used in the book was close to **accurate**.

Verne's writing inspired a Russian teacher, Konstantin Tsiolkovsky. He used math and **physics** to study how rockets worked. In 1903, he published a formula that's still used by engineers today.

German physicist Hermann Oberth also read Verne's novel. Using math and physics, he designed a **multi-stage rocket**. He launched his first rocket near Berlin, Germany, on May 7, 1931. Oberth worked with rockets for many years for Germany and the United States.

SCIENCE IN ACTION

Both Tsiolkovsky and Oberth worked with mathematical formulas, and today's rocket scientists do, too. A formula is a mathematical rule or fact shown in symbols.

Tsiolkovsky and Oberth are considered two of the fathers of modern rocket science. They used science and math to turn fiction into fact.

KONSTANTIN TSIOLKOVSKY

HERMANN OBERTH

11

THE FIRST AMERICAN ROCKET SCIENTIST

As a boy, Dr. Robert Goddard read *The War of the Worlds* by H.G. Wells and dreamed about making a vehicle that could travel to Mars. Later, as a physicist and inventor, he worked toward that dream.

On March 16, 1926, Dr. Goddard launched the first rocket that used liquid fuel. Solid rocket fuel burns all at once. With liquid fuel, adjustments can be made to control the fuel and the thrust.

Dr. Goddard proved that a rocket didn't need air to work in space. He thought about ways that a rocket might reach the moon. In 1929, Dr. Goddard put the first scientific payload on a rocket. He also figured out how to steer rockets in flight. Later rocket scientists used Dr. Goddard's ideas as they got ready to explore space.

SCIENCE IN ACTION

The first scientific payload on a rocket was a camera and a barometer. A barometer is a tool that measures air pressure.

NASA's Goddard Space Flight Center is named after Dr. Robert Goddard. Many rocket scientists work at this research center in Greenbelt, Maryland.

DR. ROBERT GODDARD

A MISSION TO MARS

Early rocket scientists dreamed of sending a person to the moon. Now, rocket scientists are planning to send people to Mars.

Will humans land on Mars? Dr. Patrick Troutman, who works at NASA's Langley Research Center in Hampton, Virginia, hopes so. He designs systems to help people explore space. He works on the rockets that lift people off the ground, the propulsion systems that get them where they want to go, and the **habitats** that keep them alive on the journey.

Dr. Troutman worked on the design of the ISS before he began his current project. He's now the lead engineer on the team that's planning to send humans to Mars. If you become a rocket scientist like Dr. Troutman, you could help people travel to other planets!

Dr. Troutman said he became a rocket scientist because "exploration of space is the only way to assure humanity will survive in the long run." He's helped push space exploration forward through his work on projects such as the creation of the ISS and NASA's mission to send astronauts to Mars.

The first human flight to Mars is planned for the 2030s. Before that, NASA is planning to send astronauts to an **asteroid** by 2025.

WORKING WITH LASERS

Men aren't the only people making a difference as rocket scientists. Many women have important jobs in this field, too. For example, Julie Williams-Byrd works as an electro-optics engineer at NASA's Langley Research Center. Electro-optics is a branch of physics that deals with the relationship between electric fields and light. Part of her job deals with the creation, testing, and operation of **lasers** carried by rockets into space. Williams-Byrd watched her lasers go up on several Space Shuttle missions. She also designed a laser for the CALIPSO satellite that's studying Earth's climate from space.

SCIENCE IN ACTION

Have you seen a laser pointer? It's a device that allows people to use NASA technology in everyday life. Dentists, surgeons, and eye doctors all use lasers, too.

Williams-Byrd wants young people to understand the importance of STEM subjects: science, technology, engineering, and math. She believes her confidence at work comes from her background in physics and math.

JULIE WILLIAMS-BYRD

16

As a team leader in NASA's Space Missions Analysis Branch, Williams-Byrd's current job is to develop and test communication technologies that will help humans get to the moon, Mars, and beyond.

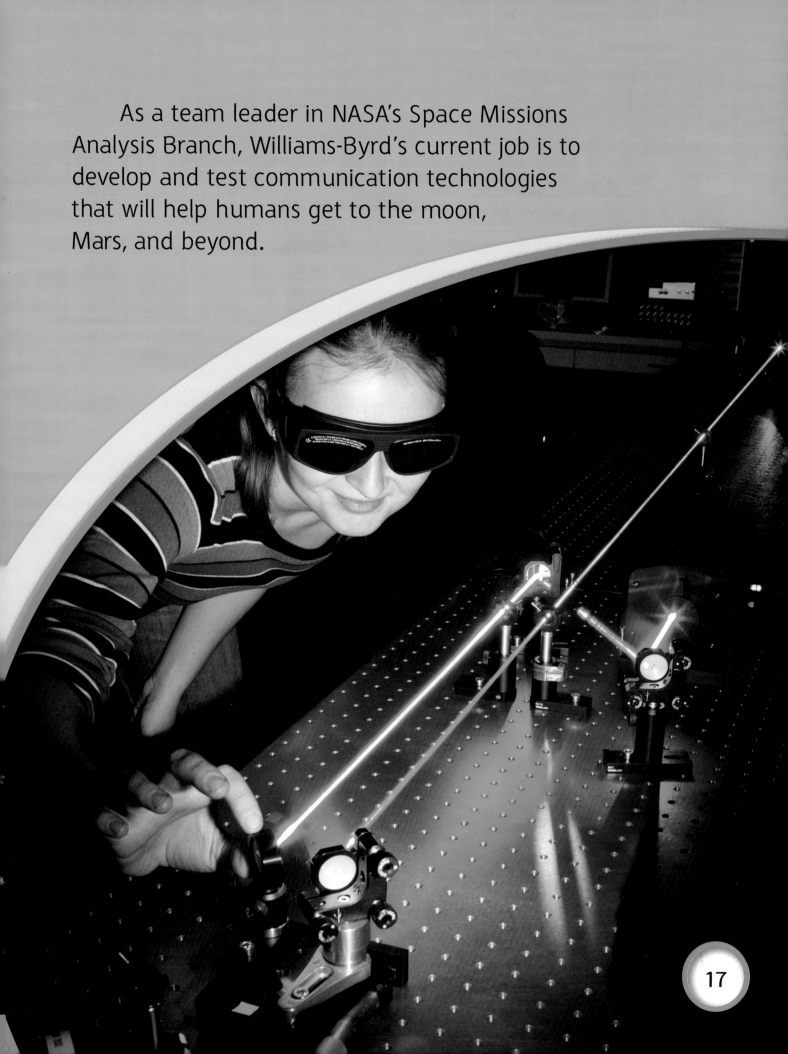

FROM WATCHING TO CREATING

Not all rocket scientists work for NASA. Dr. Dieter Zube works with spacecraft propulsion technology at a rocket propulsion manufacturer called Aerojet Rocketdyne. Dr. Zube remembers watching the first moon landing on July 20, 1969, when he was a boy. Then, his math and physics teacher took him to an open house at a nearby engineering university. Those two events inspired him to become an aerospace engineer. Now, he leads a team that researches, designs, and tests rocket engines that send people and satellites into space.

Dr. Zube runs "lifetests" to make sure the engine thrusters work correctly for the entire life of the spacecraft. He does much of his work on a computer, so if you like designing machines on computers, you might follow in his footsteps someday.

SCIENCE IN ACTION

A spacecraft needs huge, powerful engines in order to get to space. However, once in space, smaller engines control the orbit, help a spacecraft dock with the ISS, and get a spacecraft in position for reentry into Earth's atmosphere.

Dr. Zube wanted to become a rocket scientist after seeing the first moon landing. Now, his work might inspire young people to become rocket scientists!

TAKING STUFF INTO SPACE

Many people propose projects or experiments to conduct aboard the ISS. These projects and experiments all require materials and tools, which are also known as payload, that need to be sent into space. It's a rocket scientist's job to figure out how to successfully get payloads into space.

Dr. Carrie Olsen works at NASA's Marshall Spaceflight Center in Huntsville, Alabama. She directs the team that finds out what payload the experiments call for and explains to the astronauts what they have to do with the payload they're working with. She helps people design their payloads to make sure the payloads will fly successfully and be safe for the astronauts to work with.

Dr. Olsen said the hardest part of the job is getting things right the first time. "There's no second chance. Every pound going to the ISS costs thousands of dollars."

SCIENCE IN ACTION

Rocket scientists aren't the only people who combine a love of science with an interest in space. Astronauts on the ISS conduct many scientific experiments. They also test materials and technology that may be used for longer human flights.

Dr. Olsen enjoys working with people all over the world—and in orbit! She uses her science and engineering skills to be a successful leader at NASA.

THE FUTURE OF AEROSPACE ENGINEERING

Dr. Franklin Chang-Díaz spent over 1,600 hours in space on seven Space Shuttle flights. He's also a rocket scientist with a degree in plasma physics. When he retired from NASA, he founded the Ad Astra Rocket Company. Dr. Chang-Díaz is now developing a new type of rocket engine to be used on long spaceflights that carry people.

Until 2004, the U.S. government sponsored and paid for all space flights. Then, the Ansari family offered a $10 million prize to anyone who could design, build, and fly a privately funded spaceship. Aerospace engineer Burt Rutan and millionaire Paul Allen teamed up. Their SpaceShipOne won the prize. Businessman Richard Branson then bought a license to use the technology. He used it to start Virgin Galactic, which is a space tourism company. A new era in spaceflight began!

SCIENCE IN ACTION

Plasma is a collection of charged particles that's like a gas but can carry electricity and is affected by magnets. Dr. Chang-Díaz developed ways to use plasma in rocket propulsion.

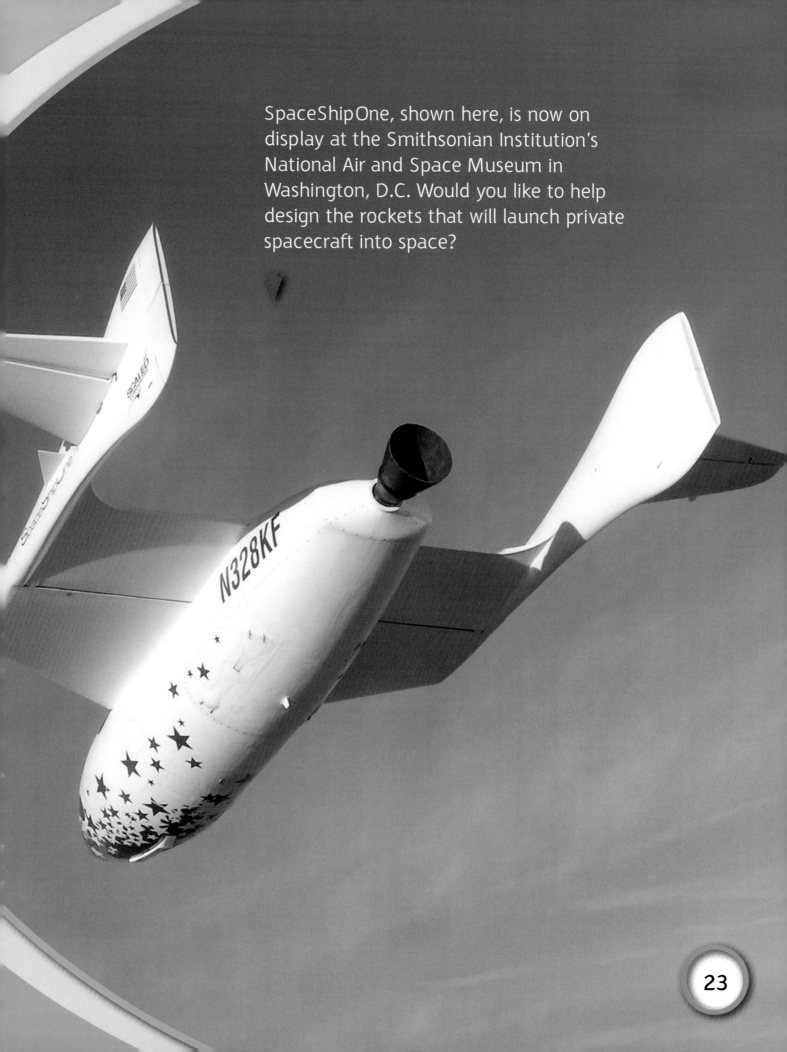

SpaceShipOne, shown here, is now on display at the Smithsonian Institution's National Air and Space Museum in Washington, D.C. Would you like to help design the rockets that will launch private spacecraft into space?

KEEP ON STUDYING!

If you plan to become a rocket scientist, you'll need a solid background in math and science. Since writing letters, papers, and articles is a big part of the job, you'll also need excellent writing skills. Take as many classes in these areas as you can from now through high school.

Then, keep on studying! You'll need at least a bachelor's degree—or a four-year college degree—to become a rocket scientist. However, most rocket scientists have either a master's degree or a doctorate, which are both advanced degrees that require more time in school.

You may be able to get a summer job in this field as an intern. You may also start a full-time job with a bachelor's degree and get your advanced degree while you're working. In some cases, you may even get paid to go to school.

SCIENCE IN ACTION

Internships give students a chance to see how the things they learn in the classroom are applied in the working world. An intern generally works for a period of time in their chosen field of study for little or no pay in order to gain experience.

Think of these subjects as tools in your toolbox for a career as a rocket scientist. Once you know the basics, you can use them to learn even more!

math

writing

foreign languages

What should you study?

computer-aided design

computer science

science
(astronomy, biology, chemistry, physics)

COLLEGE STUDENTS LAUNCH EXPERIMENTS

On August 12, 2015, cheers went up as a sounding rocket blasted into the air from NASA's Wallops Flight Facility in Virginia. College students from across the United States watched as the payload for their experiments soared 97 miles (156.1 km) into the air and then **parachuted** safely into the Atlantic Ocean.

One team's 3-D printer worked during the flight. Another team used smartphones and smartwatches to communicate with their instrument. A third made a heater that melted and mixed two metals that can't combine in Earth's gravity.

Jesse Austin, the student program manager for this project, gave this advice to kids interested in science: "Don't be afraid to get good grades. Don't worry if kids make fun of you. I never thought I'd be working on space stuff, and now my friends are blown away."

SCIENCE IN ACTION

Sounding rockets are rockets used to try out new techniques—or methods—and instruments. The results help rocket scientists develop new space technology.

Shown here are some of the students involved in the sounding rocket launch at NASA's Wallops Flight Facility on August 12, 2015. More than 60 people participated in this project.

HIGH SCHOOL ROCKET SCIENTISTS

Your introduction to rocket science could start sooner than you think! Each year, high school students all over the country spend time at NASA facilities.

In August 2015, a group of tenth-grade students from Virginia lived and worked at NASA's Wallops Flight Facility for a week. Working with rocket scientists, teachers, and college assistants, they developed a space mission based on real missions. They toured the control room and the launch pads, and they saw an Antares rocket being built. A highlight of the week was watching a rocket launch.

If you dream of being a rocket scientist, you can also gain valuable experience at a summer science camp. You might make new friends who are interested in this exciting career, too.

SCIENCE IN ACTION

Every state has a Space Grant Consortium to support educational opportunities for students interested in STEM careers with NASA. Search online for the one from your state, and find out what high school and college programs are available for you to take part in someday.

Students who took part in the week at NASA's
Wallops Flight Facility got to see how science is
applied outside the classroom during such extreme
events as a rocket launch!

ALL SYSTEMS GO!

A career as a rocket scientist involves lots of long hours and patience. Working with rockets can be dangerous, or unsafe. You might travel frequently and be away from home for extended periods of time. However, rocket scientists know the time and effort they put into their work creates the future of space travel. They're changing how we explore space—one rocket launch at a time.

If you're interested in this extreme career path, take Dr. Olsen's advice: "There are so many careers that you can't even imagine exist. If you think you are interested, get a foundation in math, physics, and chemistry. Then, find out what those things can be used for." With that foundation, a whole world of careers in rocket science will be open to you!

GLOSSARY

accurate: Free of mistakes.

asteroid: A small, rocky body in space.

GPS: A radio system that uses satellites to tell you where you are and to give you directions to other places.

habitat: The place where a person lives.

International Space Station: A space station in low Earth orbit where astronauts live and work.

laser: A device that produces a narrow beam of light.

multi-stage rocket: A rocket that uses two or more engines— each with its own fuel—that fire one after the other.

parachute: To fall slowly back to the ground using something shaped like an umbrella.

physics: The branch of science that deals with matter and energy, as well as how they interact.

probe: An unmanned craft used to send information about a body in space back to Earth.

satellite: A spacecraft placed in orbit around Earth, a moon, or a planet to collect information or for communication.

vehicle: A machine used to carry goods or people from one place to another.

wind tunnel: A long, narrow room used to test the effects of wind on aircraft, spacecraft, and other vehicles.

INDEX

WEBSITES

Due to the changing nature of Internet links, PowerKids Press has developed an online list of websites related to the subject of this book. This site is updated regularly. Please use this link to access the list: www.powerkidslinks.com/exsci/rocket